Enjoy!

R.W.B.

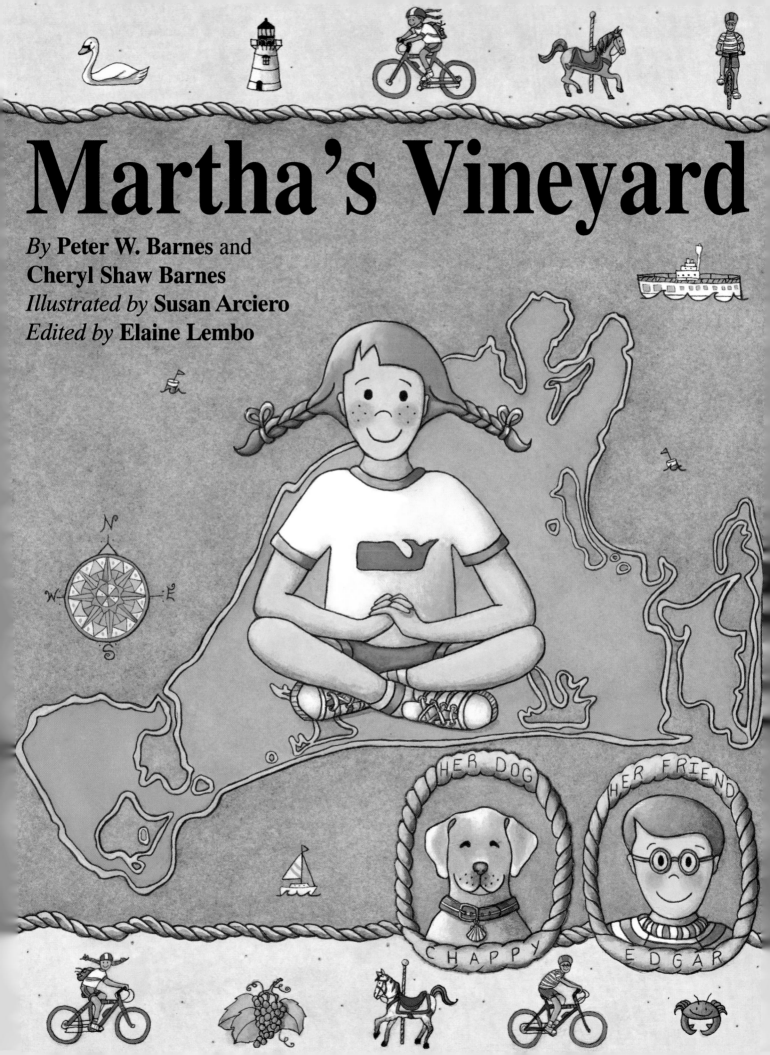

Martha's Vineyard

By **Peter W. Barnes** and
Cheryl Shaw Barnes
Illustrated by **Susan Arciero**
Edited by **Elaine Lembo**

HER DOG

CHAPPY

HER FRIEND

EDGAR

First Edition

ISBN 0-9637688-3-2

Library of Congress Catalog Card Number: 95-90166

10 9 8 7 6 5 4 3 2 1

Rosebud Books are published by: Vacation Spot Publishing
P.O. Box 17011
Alexandria, Virginia 22302

Printed in the United States of America

*This book is dedicated to everyone who
has ever lived in or visited Martha's Vineyard
and fallen in love with this wonderful island,
and to the other special Martha in our lives,
our sister, Martha Shaw Whitley.*
—P.W.B. and C.S.B.

To Cletus and Eric, for your love and support.
—S.A.
To Rick, my man of the sea.
—E.L.

Martha Murphy Applebee
Lives her life so Vineyardly,
On her island, in the ocean,
That she loves with great devotion.

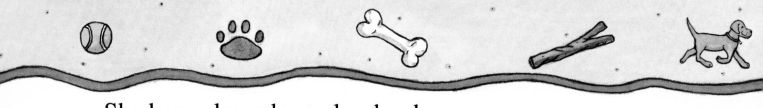

She has a dog who makes her happy,
  A labrador, whose name is Chappy—
Short for Chappaquiddick—and
  He loves to swim, then roll in sand.

Edgar Towne is Martha's friend;
    He sees her riding 'round the bend.
"Martha, Martha, wait for me!"
    He shouts to Martha, eagerly.

Martha says, "No time to waste—
I'm going to my special place!
It's down the road, beyond a care.
Now come along! I'll take you there!"

So off they ride, down-islandly,
Beyond the old Pagoda Tree,

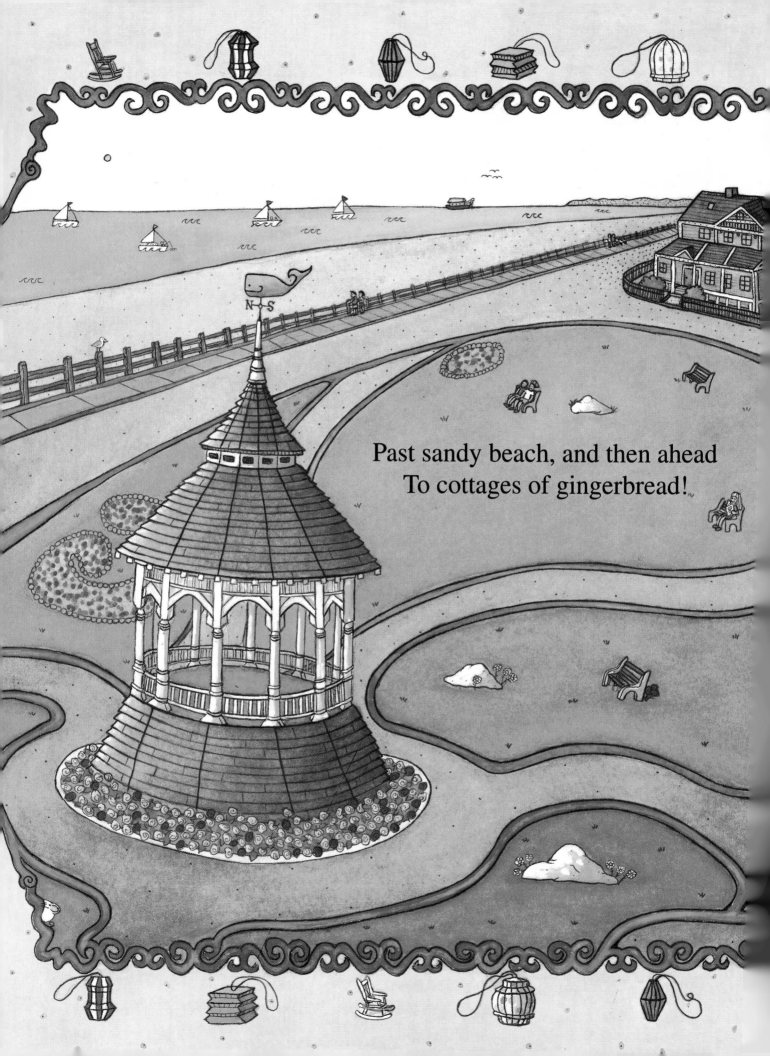

Past sandy beach, and then ahead
To cottages of gingerbread!

They ride the ride than never ends,
    For Martha, Edgar and their friends.
Around and 'round the horses fly—
    Now grab the ring as you go by!

A lighthouse stands majestically
To bring home sailors out at sea,
To welcome friends both far and near,
Day after day, year after year.

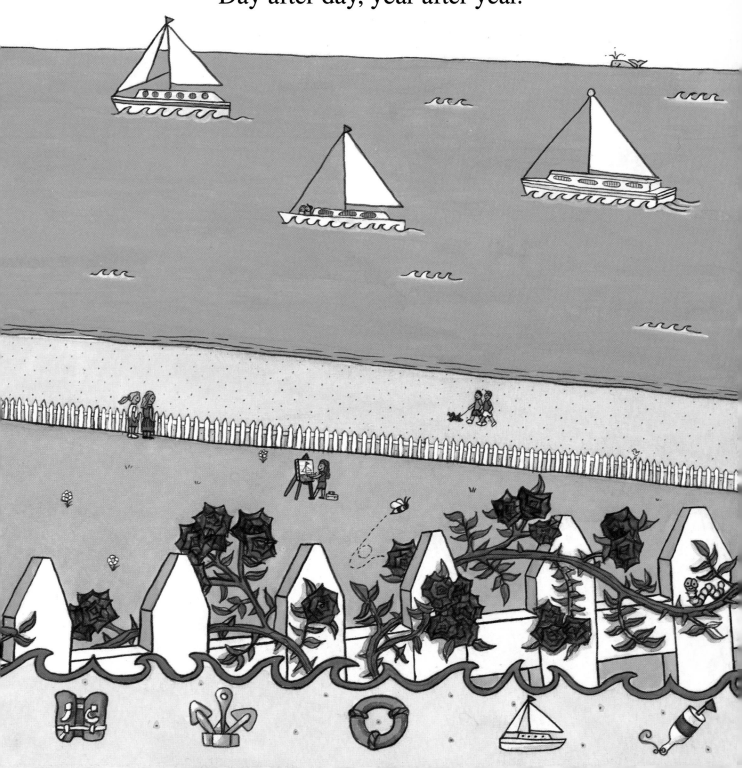

West Tisbury is always where
  The Vineyard holds its summer fair.
Chappy makes a friend or two—
  Some crow, some oink, some baa, some moo.

Next they go to play among
    The woods at Corner Beetlebung.
"Olly, olly, oxen free!"
    Martha shouts behind a tree.

There's a beach plum—and another!
Martha picks them for her mother,
To make a beach plum jam delight
When Martha takes them home tonight.

They pedal on to old Gay Head
    With cliffs of orange, yellow, red.
Indian gods, in days of old,
    Made their home there, so it's told.

Edgar says to Martha, "So,
    Just how much further must we go?
Just where is this special place?"
    As back to Martha's house they race.

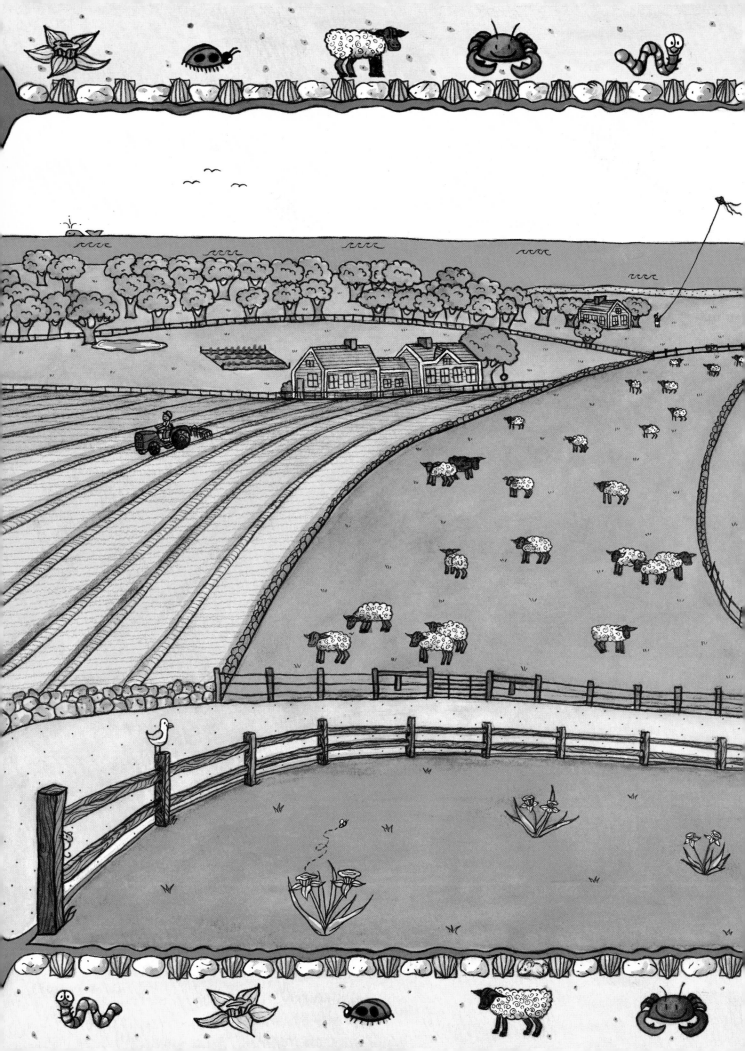

She says to Edgar, Vineyardly,
    "You silly boy! Why, don't you see?
Each beach, each town, each smiling face—
The Vineyard IS my special place!"

Historical Notes for Parents and Teachers

Martha's Vineyard was formed during the Great Ice Age, from the rock and "till" mixture of soil and gravel left by melting glaciers. Native Americans were the first inhabitants. In 1602, explorer Bartholomew Gosnold named the island for his daughter, Martha, and the wild grapevines he found there.

The first English settlers arrived in the mid-1600s and put down roots in what is now Edgartown, where Martha, Edgar and Chappy begin their adventure. Chappy's name is derived from Chappaquiddick Island, just across the water from Edgartown.

The old Pagoda tree the children ride past is on South Water Street. It was planted by Captain Thomas Milton, who brought it from China as a seedling in the 1800s. The gingerbread cottages they ride to next are in Oak Bluffs. The town is also the home of the famous Flying Horses carousel, which is more than a hundred years old and is a national landmark.

The children visit the East Chop Lighthouse, one of two that guard the entrance to Vineyard Haven Harbor. Vineyard Haven is the main port for the ferries that travel between the island and the mainland. There are three other lighthouses on the Vineyard.

Then the children ride to the Agriculture Fair in West Tisbury, held in late summer. On the way out of town, they go to Beetlebung Corner. The trees there are Tupelos, but islanders named them "Beetlebungs" because their extremely hard wood made them good for making mallets (called "beetles") and stoppers (called "bungs") for barrels. Next, Martha and Edgar pick beach plums near Menemsha, a fishing village on the west side of the island.

In Gay Head, the children view the beautiful, bright cliffs. They are made of layers of sands, gravels and clays laid down millions of years ago. According to Native American legend, the Indian god Moshup lived in the cliffs with his family. On their way back to Edgartown, the children ride through West Tisbury.

For more information on Martha's Vineyard, contact or visit the Duke's County Historical Society.